T0208545

For Who Hath
—**Resisted**—
His Will

His Will, His Word, His Grace

K E N N E T H   L .   R A V E N

WESTBOW
P R E S S
A DIVISION OF THOMAS NELSON

Copyright © 2013 Kenneth L. Raven.
Cover artwork by Sharon M. Raven.

All rights reserved. No part of this book may be used or reproduced by
any means, graphic, electronic, or mechanical, including photocopying,
recording, taping or by any information storage retrieval system
without the written permission of the publisher except in the case
of brief quotations embodied in critical articles and reviews.

WestBow Press books may be ordered through booksellers or by contacting:

WestBow Press
A Division of Thomas Nelson
1663 Liberty Drive
Bloomington, IN 47403
www.westbowpress.com
1 (866) 928-1240

Unless otherwise noted, all Scripture quotations are from, the text
conformable to that of the edition of 1611 commonly known as the Authorized
or King James Bible, Published by Local Church Bible Publishers.

Because of the dynamic nature of the Internet, any web addresses or
links contained in this book may have changed since publication and
may no longer be valid. The views expressed in this work are solely those
of the author and do not necessarily reflect the views of the publisher,
and the publisher hereby disclaims any responsibility for them.

ISBN: 978-1-4908-1315-8 (sc)
ISBN: 978-1-4908-1317-2 (hc)
ISBN: 978-1-4908-1316-5 (e)

Library of Congress Control Number: 2013918646

Printed in the United States of America.

WestBow Press rev. date: 10/22/2013

Contents

Acknowledgments

To the many who have come before me and who are working even now with Jesus Christ, leading His lambs to victory.

To my wife Sharon, who has not only supported me but joins me daily in worshiping Him who is able. My loving daughter Angela and family who have been a constant joy to me. And my dear friends in Christ, Scott and Krista Boehman for their steadfast loyalty and support.

Introduction

Flesh versus Spirit

Having never attempted to write anything other than a sermon or a letter, I find I am urged to do so now by the same Spirit who leads me to put the Lord Christ Jesus first in my life.

As I write this introduction, I am fully aware this world wants a king. Israel demanded a king and rejected God (1 Samuel 8). Israel had forsaken God and served other gods. We need to understand how the true King, Jesus Christ, was and is received here on earth. He was rejected and crucified.

You see, those belonging to this world can never know Him. "And this is life eternal, that they might know thee the only true God, and Jesus Christ, whom thou has sent"

(John 17:3). Only the world of true believers is able to discern the truth, which sets them free from the world of flesh.

Even as I write, the world displays a cult like worship in a false hope that some other can give them happiness, peace and prosperity. Instead of the Lamb of God, meek and humble to the end, unbelievers seek the things of this world. Natural man is self-righteous and self-serving to the end. "The LORD hath made all *things* for himself: yea, even the wicked for the day of evil. Every one *that is* proud in heart *is* an abomination to the LORD: *though* hand *join* in hand, he shall not be unpunished" (Proverbs 16:4–5).

Life can never deny the Creator control of that which He created for a purpose only He knows. My hope in writing this book is to use the Word of God to enlighten those who claim their free will as a part of their salvation, to understand, "Salvation is of the Lord!"

"NOW faith is the substance of things hoped for, the evidence of things not seen" (Hebrews 11:1). May God speak to your hearts; I would not ask anyone what faith you are, Baptist, Catholic or any other. Faith is not the name of a religion; faith is a gift of God. "So then faith *cometh* by hearing, and hearing by the word of God" (Romans 10:17). Were you born a Baptist, a Catholic or even a Christian? No, you were born a sinner. Being born of God is completely a different matter than a man's physical birth. Jesus Christ emphatically declares in John 3:3, "Verily, verily, I say unto thee, Except a man be born again, he cannot see the kingdom of God."

If given five seconds to say anything to those lost souls, I would give them the same message Jeremiah and the prophets declared: turn toward the Lord before it's too late!

This book is a cry from the wilderness of this world for those in this world to turn from fads and fables. Turn to the truth that only God is in control; only He can cause a true change in us. It is God who draws His children to Jesus.

Doing the Will of God

Not a man-made church, not a man-made will, but only by the will of God.

We, like Jesus, are here not to do our will but to do the will of the Father. "Which were born, not of blood, nor of the will of the flesh, nor of the will of man, but of God" (John 1:13).

To be like Jesus, we are no longer concerned with our own will, but rather, we are led by the Spirit.

Jesus said, "I can of mine own self do nothing: as I hear, I judge: and my judgment is just; because I seek not mine own will, but the will of the Father which hath sent me" (John 5:30).

Jesus prayed, "O my Father, if it be possible, let this cup pass from me: nevertheless not as I will but as thou *wilt*" (Matthew 26:39).

Do we serve our Father or ourselves? His will is always righteous while ours is always selfish.

The sinner, drawn by the Father, cries out, "Have Thine own way, Lord. Have Thine own way. Thou art the Potter; I am the clay."[1] The man of flesh, however, believes God needs man's permission or acceptance to do God's will (work in him).

Someone said, "The only perfection in man is man doing God's will." This is undeniably true. Only after God's grace was given me and I became born again, a new creation, did I understand God's will for me. And this only in His Word and His Holy Spirit, who constantly shows me Jesus. "He shall glorify me: for he shall receive of mine, and shall shew *it* unto you" (John 16:14).

---

1   Christian hymn with lyrics by Adelaide A. Pollard and music by George C. Stebbins.

Chapter 1

Two Wills—Two Worlds:
Humanism vs. Theism

There Must Be a Change!

"AND you *hath he quickened*, who were dead in trespasses and sins; Wherein in time past ye walked according to the course of this world, according to the prince of the power of the air, the spirit that now worketh in the children of disobedience: Among whom also we all had our conversation in times past in the lusts of our flesh, fulfilling the desires of the flesh and of the mind; and were by nature the children of wrath, even as others" (Ephesians 2:1–3). Paul describes us as we were, before we entered the world of the beloved.

So we see the difference between the world of man's

will—the world of unbelievers—and the world of the true believer is God's will for His children. Two wills, two worlds. Oil and water will never mix. And just as Jesus turned the water into wine, He has changed the goats to lambs.

Paul declares there is a war going on within God's children. Old man, the flesh, fights for his will. However, the child of God now is able to *not* sin. It is natural man who attempts to serve two masters. He interjects himself as a co-redeemer in the sovereign work of God through His Son, Jesus Christ.

Carnal man is unable to deny his glory in himself, fixating on the acceptance of other men rather than on receiving our Lord. Yet herein the truth shall set you free. "According as he hath chosen us in him before the foundation of the world, that we should be holy and without blame before him in love: Having predestinated us unto the adoption of children by Jesus Christ to himself, according to the good pleasure of his will. To the praise of the glory of his grace, wherein he hath made us accepted in the beloved" (Ephesians 1:4–6). The children accepted in the beloved receive the grace and faith from God through our Savior, Jesus Christ.

Many people rely on a co-redeemer, and many claim their will as a part of salvation. These need only look to Jesus for salvation. It was His blood did save me, and His alone.

"And all the inhabitants of the earth *are* reputed as nothing: and he doeth according to his will in the army of heaven, and *among* the inhabitants of the earth: and none can stay his hand, or say unto him, What doest thou?" (Daniel 4:35).

The spiritual man knows the change was not forced but was a work of God, whereby irresistibly we cry, "Abba," having been given the gift of faith mentioned in Ephesians, chapter 2, a work of God in us.

Must God wait and be grateful to man for accepting? The man led by the Spirit is submissive and thankful unto the will of his Father in heaven.

A Changed Will

Oh, most sovereign and immutable Father
    in heaven,
I shan't ask you why,
But in my heart I find anew
A loving Spirit that is true.

A new man I come now
To you, Lord, to worship and bow.
My will I no longer care
For it is your will has brought me here.

How I love you, how I serve you,
I pray you tell me,
For it is that, I love to do,
Sealed to that day of redemption, by you.

In the book of Ecclesiastes, Solomon declares that there is "nothing new under the sun," meaning there is nothing one can do that hasn't already been done, nothing one can see that hasn't already been seen and so on. And although I believe this to be reality, I also know that to every individual, each thought and each day is a new experience.

However, after being drawn to Jesus by His Father, our perspective is different. In God's will, we see that the cause and effect of everything is to His purpose. God's love is dependent on no one, and nothing reigns above His sovereignty. Even His unmerited favor, grace, is bestowed on those He chooses. It is free grace given to the bride-elect.

God's grace changes our entire being. It's no longer our free will, but His will be done, as Jesus said. "For I came down from heaven, not to do mine own will, but the will of him that sent me" (John 6:38). It is our position in Christ that changes our will to God's will in us.

Being drawn by God definitely results in salvation for the elect. Many people try to define the word *draw* to mean "woo" the natural man to Jesus, but I believe the true meaning is "to drag." Then carnal man would say, "What about my free will? Does God bring a man kicking and screaming to be born again?"

To this, I answer, Paul didn't want to be a Christian. He hated Christians! It was *against his will* to be a Christian! Newborn babies always kick and scream as they leave what to them seems a safe haven. Paul wasn't wooed off his horse. I'm sure his experience on the road to Damascus was a change he neither wanted nor was willing to accept. But at the appointed time, God draws whom He will, and

His sheep come, being convicted by the Holy Spirit. Jesus declares, "My sheep hear my voice, and I know them, and they follow me" (John 10:27).

It was "my will" that kept me in bondage. Having my eyes opened for the first time, I was drawn by the Father to the Son. "No man can come to me, except the Father which hath sent me draw him: and I will raise him up at the last day" (John 6:44). We were dead in our trespasses until God drew us to Jesus and we received the free gift.

"As thou hast given him power over all flesh, that he should give eternal life to as many as thou hast given him" (John 17:2).

Naturally Inclined

Free will is natural; giving up that will is a work of God. Only if a man is enabled by God can he see the root of all false doctrine is *legality*, a doctrine of salvation by works. Those believing in a doctrine wherein man must persevere of his own self have no freedom, no joy. He must rely and hope on his own merits, not trusting completely in our Lord. Works become his hope in Christ. The law must keep him, not grace; the law, not God's love.

At the new birth, our will having changed, we follow Jesus. We are free, indeed! Our self-centered desires are nailed to the cross along with our rebellious free will. Having freedom in Christ, we are beloved of God, born of God, and taught of God.

Charles H. Spurgeon, (1834–1892) was a noted

theologian and pastor and has been called the prince of preachers. He stated, "I must confess that I never would have been saved if I could have helped it. As long as I could, I rebelled and revolted and struggled against God. When he would have me pray, I would not pray. When he would have me listen to the sound of the ministry, I would not. And when I heard, and the tear rolled down my cheek, I wiped it away and defied him to melt my heart. Then he gave me the effectual blow of grace, and there was no resisting that irresistible effort. It conquered my depraved will and made me bow myself before the scepter of his grace.

And so it is in every case. Man revolts against his Savior, but where God determines to save, save he will. God never was thwarted yet in any one of his purposes. Man does resist with all his might, but all the might of man, tremendous though it be for sin, is not equal to the majestic might of the Most High."[2]

As a child of God, I know it was not free will, but free grace which is unmerited favor that saved me and gave me faith that I would not accept, yet received.

Spurgeon was so enlightened in God's doctrine of grace as to declare it, saying, "There is no soul living who holds more firmly to the doctrine of grace than I do, and if any man asks me whether I am ashamed to be called a Calvinist, I answer, I wish to be called nothing but a

---

2   Tom Carter, Compiler, 2200 Quotations from the Writings of Charles H. Spurgeon, Grand Rapids, MI: Baker Book House Co, 1988, 89.

Christian; but if you ask me if I hold to the doctrinal views which were held by John Calvin? I reply, I do in the main hold of them, and rejoice to avow."[3]

The man who adds anything else to the work on the cross of Christ, I fear, denies the power of the blood alone for redemption. There is no other way, no other reason that His love for us be made manifest in us for His glory to His purpose. Ask me how and I will tell you, "Nothing but the Blood of Jesus."[4]

Jesus is talking to believers when He says, "And ye shall know the truth, and the truth shall make you free" (John 8:32).

In verse 33, we find these men not understanding. They answer Jesus by stating they never were in bondage to anyone. And since they are free men with free will, how can Jesus say, "Ye shall be made free?"

In verse 36, Jesus tells them, "If the Son therefore shall make you free, ye shall be free indeed."

And here comes the real truth about their free will. Look at verse 38, where we find out about our will and just whose will it is that we serve. "I speak that of which I have seen with my Father: and ye do that which ye have seen with your father."

Read and follow the Word. "I am the light of the world: he that followeth me shall not walk in darkness, but shall have the light of life" (John 8:12).

---

3   Spurgeongems.org., A Defense of Calvinism, volume 7, 6.

4   Words and music: Robert Lowry

Have you ever wondered why the world can't understand God's will? Why it is they believe their salvation rests on their free will and not His? You have only to look at His words, and you who are His sheep will hear and understand. "Why do ye not understand my speech? *even* because ye cannot hear my word" (John 8:43). And "Ye are of *your* father the devil, and the lusts of your father ye will do" (John 8:44).

And here is the conclusion of this matter. In this same gospel, Jesus says, "He that is of God heareth God's words: ye therefore hear *them* not, because ye are not of God" (John 8:47). You may call this foolishness or a stumbling block, but to the elect, it is honey from the lips of God.

I can persuade no man, for it is a work of God. As King Agrippa told Paul, "Paul, Almost thou persuadest me to be a Christian" (Acts 26:28). Almost a Christian is not a Christian at all. Saved is saved or not. Salvation that can be lost is not salvation of the Lord. A carnal salvation of man is found in man's will. It is in man's will that we find the sin problem.

The Bible declares, "No man can serve two masters" (Matthew 6:24). Will is never pure unless we are bond servants to Him whose will is perfect and made perfect in His own.

Our attitudes paint pictures in our minds. Without Jesus, we have only our free will, and our free will changes with each breath we take. Man shall never find freedom within his will, nor will he find God's will. Hence he is enslaved and held in bondage.

Martin Luther said, "If any man doth ascribe aught of salvation, even the very least, to the *free will* of man, he knoweth nothing of grace, and he hath not learnt Jesus Christ aright."[5]

True freedom is freedom in Christ Jesus, wherein our will is broken and we are able to do the will of God. The things of this world become smaller compared to His love for us. Problems are only problems if you perceive them as such. Whatever you give attention to, you make important.

While looking for the land of milk and honey, the Promised Land, Caleb said, "Let us go up at once, and possess it; for we are well able to overcome it" (Numbers 13:30). Other scouts saw giants as obstacles too big to overcome. (See Numbers 13:33.) Don't focus on your enemies and what they do. Don't make them bigger than they are.

God's people believe and obey and are able to understand. "Not that I speak in respect of want: for I have learned, in whatsoever state I am, *therewith* to be content" (Philippians 4:11). This is an example of walking in faith to His purpose.

To be happy in Jesus is to trust and obey. The old hymn denotes obeying God's will, not trusting our own. This new creature, born of God, is no longer chained by Satan to a will of sin.

---

5   sermonindex.net

Living a Lie

A true passion for Jesus will never be shown to us in a movie, as we are to worship Him in truth and spirit. To demonstrate a mock beating of one impersonating Christ is purely humanism.

There are actually only two religions, humanism and Christian theism.

Humanism is of and for man's glory. This seems right to man, but in the end looks to the ways of man, not God. "There is a way which seemeth right unto a man, but the end thereof *are* the ways of death" (Proverbs 14:12).

Theism, to me, is of and for God's glory alone. This term was first used by Ralph Cudworth (1617–1688). He described a theist as one who believes that a perfectly conscious, understanding being or mind, existing of itself from eternity, was the cause of all other things. A true believer knows this being is God, through His Son, Jesus Christ. "For my thoughts *are* not your thoughts, neither *are* your ways my ways, saith the LORD" (Isaiah 55:8).

The Bible makes a clear distinction between humanism and Christian theism. Many churches practice humanism; each forms its own doctrines or beliefs from parts of the Bible so as to be different. Much as in politics, they end up trying to please man and changing with any new fad that comes along. And they call this "progressive." We see man serving himself in the flesh, instead of man serving and worshiping the Lord, God of all things.

Many church billboards advertise musical groups,

Easter egg hunts, and so on as reasons why people should come to hear about Jesus. Fellowship is not the cause or reason for worship. Rather, we come together and together we worship, united in Christ Jesus. But many will murmur and wag their tongues, declaring fellowship is entertainment. Their church must have basketball for the kids and a music ministry and something for everyone.

God's church does have something for everyone, and His name is Jesus. He alone satisfies our every need. We worship in Spirit and truth. A true thirst for His Word causes true fellowship, which is holy and respectful. But to the many, it's not enough. This world has them mesmerized.

"Which denomination are you?" people ask me.

I answer, "None of man's denominations, for by God's own sovereign grace and the faith given me, I hear my Shepherd call. I am a Christian, and only to His doctrine do I answer."

The elect worship in Spirit and truth. Natural man must have something physical as well as tangible to worship. (See Exodus 20:4.)

———

Another demand of humanism is a sign. The Pharisees needed a sign; thus they did not recognize Jesus as the Son of God. "Then said Jesus unto him, Except ye see signs and wonders, ye will not believe" (John 4:48).

The beloved recognize Jesus Christ as their Lord and Savior as well as the Good Shepherd and love of their lives.

In the gospel of John, chapter 8 alone is a great proof of opposing views between two worlds, which are flesh and spirit. For many know the Devil, but few are chosen to know Jesus Christ.

While unbelievers search for a sign, it is God's sovereign grace that is the efficacious and irresistible call the regenerate receive. The elect not only know Jesus as Savior, but indeed receive Him in the Holy Spirit.

The Door

Oh Lord, that the door be a great sea divided
Perhaps a dirty manger harboring lost sheep
Thou keepest the door opened or closed
Causing us to awaken or sleep

In your Spirit lies our life itself
That life-giving blood does wash us clean
Thank you, God, for the gift, the door
And for your Spirit that keeps me evermore

There is more to say
And much to do
But nothing that calms me
As the door to you

Humanism

Natural man is without the Spirit of God, and so he remains under the law. Not knowing the grace of God, he lives under the cloud of the law, where no spiritual light shines. Neither can he keep the law. The Bible says, "Knowing this, that the law is not made for a righteous man, but for the lawless and disobedient, for the ungodly and for sinners, for unholy and profane, for murderers of fathers and murderers of mothers, for manslayers" (1 Timothy 1:9). Since natural man relies on his own free will, his own faith, and his own perseverance he remains under the law. Because he puts his trust in himself rather than looking to Jesus Christ for salvation, he is a vessel unto destruction.

Recently, I heard a popular television evangelist declare, "I got myself saved." If indeed he *got himself* saved, nothing happened. His reasoning is of the flesh. Except for the grace of God, no one has saving faith; thus, he can't know Jesus Christ as his Savior.

We read in 1 Corinthians 15:10, "But by the grace of God I am what I am: and his grace which *was bestowed* upon me was not in vain; but I laboured more abundantly than they all: yet not I, but the grace of God which was with me."

In chapter 6 of the gospel of John, Jesus declares, "No one can come to me, except the Father which hath sent me draw him: and I will raise him up at the last day" (v. 44). "And he said, Therefore said I unto you, that no man can come unto me, except it were given unto him of my Father" (v. 65).

When the vessel of destruction hears God's doctrine, he resists and walks no more with Jesus. We understand that many who claim Jesus will recant. "From that *time* many of his disciples went back, and walked no more with him" (John 6:66).

A child of God receives the spirit of God indwelling within and relies solely on our Lord's righteousness. Thus, his reasoning comes from God's Word. Being born again, he is in the covenant of grace. Jesus Christ is the propitiation for his sins. And it's our position in Christ by which we are justified.

To carnal man, humanism looks right, even holy. But it's born out of *self-righteous* pride and goes against God's immutable Word. The worldly have only their decision to justify their motives. At the root of humanism and man's free will is found pride.

For instance, to a humanist *receiving* God now means *accepting* God. But between the two there is a grave difference. Humanism simply changes the words to accommodate man's part in his salvation. It is Christ's work on the cross for the elect that we look to. This is true and this is doctrine. Amen.

"For the time will come when they will not endure sound doctrine; but after their own lusts shall they heap to themselves teachers, having itching ears; And they shall turn away *their* ears from the truth, and shall be turned unto fables" (2 Timothy 4:3–4).

God's grace is for natural man resistible; "For they that are after the flesh do mind the things of the flesh; but they that are after the Spirit the things of the Spirit" (Romans 8:5).

Flesh can only know *common grace.*

But to the sheep belonging to Jesus, able to hear the Spirit, *uncommon grace* is an irresistible call from our heavenly Father. In Romans 9:19, Paul asks, "For who hath resisted his will?"

Humanists, much like the Pharisees, won't put up with the true children of God. Their religion is of man. And although they claim God as their Father and Jesus as the Savior, it is a different gospel they hear. A different gospel they preach. A different Jesus they want. They desire a Christ who serves the world, a world that will pass away.

While many profess Jesus as Lord and Savior, they don't know the true Jesus. Proof lies in their relationship with Him. In many churches, we hear many prayers concerning the flesh, but few about the Spirit of God. Their relationship is all about physical needs and is enveloped in their problems. Adding music and entertainment while remaining indifferent to His Word and Spirit, they walk away when the excitement is over. This comes as a result of their dependence on the flesh to believe in their own ability and that they chose Him.

God's Word says one can't come to Christ unless the Father grants it. He is calling even now. Can you hear? Do you believe that you can accept that which you have not received? If He who is able calls, you will receive. Come if you hear His words, for you have received His irresistible grace. For His sheep do come!

Let me explain. A man can't truly believe in or receive what he doesn't know. *You say you believe in Jesus Christ, I ask you, do you know Him?*

Again, all but the true church are bewitched by an untrue doctrine, in which the true Christ Jesus is confused with a worldly form of a different messiah they call Jesus. It is a doctrine in which *you accept*, making Him passive, a doctrine in which you are in control, one in which man must act on his own merit (Pelagianism)[6] or initiate the first part of his salvation (semi-Pelagianism). And yet another system of theology which makes salvation in part dependant on the free will of man is, Arminianism.[7]

The Bible declares we are spiritually dead and only Jesus can resurrect the dead. God is the Alpha and Omega. He is the beginning and the end. "Looking unto Jesus the author and finisher of *our* faith" (Hebrews 12:2).

Let us go to the graveyard and ask the dead to live. Only God is able.

---

6   Pelagius (fl. C. 390-418) was an ascetic who opposed the idea of predestination and asserted a strong version of the doctrine of free will. From the Wikipedia, the free encyclopedia

7   Jacobus Arminius (1560-1609), was a Dutch Reformed theologian and professor of theology at the University of Leiden. He is most noted for his departure from the Reformed theology of the Belgic Confession resulting in what became the Calvinist-Arminian controversy addressed at the Synod of Dort (1618-1619). theopedia.com/Jacobus_Arminius

Paul says, "Being confident of this very thing, that he which hath begun a good work in you will perform *it* until the day of Jesus Christ" (Philippians 1:6). I tell you the truth: only by the grace of God can a man persevere.

I remember hearing of a man who left his wife to go many miles away to earn money and prepare a way for them to be together forever. He said as he was leaving that he loved her and would return as soon as everything was made ready. As time went on, her friends and relatives began to have doubts about him. She told them, "You just don't know him like I do." Knowing he was a good man and knowing him personally, she believed his word given only to her. It was personal.

I tell you this story knowing that Jesus Christ is not only able, but also that He is righteous. I know Him and believe Him. To each chosen one, it's personal.

My mother and father, whom I loved, have passed. No matter how I might try to have you know them as I do in my heart, it's impossible. This personal relationship I still have with them is only for me because of my relationship to them as one of their children. Each child of God is able to share in the inheritance while each enjoys a personal relationship with Him.

Just as this world didn't know Jesus, they can't know us.

"BEHOLD, what manner of love the Father hath bestowed upon us, that we should be called the sons of God: therefore the world knoweth us not, because it knew him not" (1 John 3:1).

I remember one Sunday, while holding a worship

service at home, a friend asked about the great white throne. She wanted to know if we would all be judged there. And since the Bible declares we will all be judged by our works, she wanted to know what works counted.

The first thing that came to my mind was Hebrews 11:6 "But without faith *it is* impossible to please *him*: for he that cometh to God must believe that he is, and *that* he is a rewarder of them that diligently seek him." We won't be at the white throne of judgment. Those whose names are in the Book of Life will be judged already innocent by the blood of Jesus Christ. Our works will count only because of His work on the cross. That is, we will then be completely conformed in His image.

In the gospel of John, Jesus speaks of the work that counts. "Then said they unto him, What shall we do, that we might work the works of God? Jesus answered and said unto them, This is the work of God, that ye believe on him whom he hath sent" (John 6:28–29). And we understand it is His work in us and not our work that is done.

But the works of those judged at the white throne will be works without faith. They are works of unrighteousness, just as Cain's work didn't please God. God's election will stand and His will be done.

In the Bible, James 2:20 says, "But wilt thou know, O vain man, that faith without works is dead?" and this is true, but works pleasing to God always follow and never precede a saving faith. We also were unable to please God until the appointed time, when we received Jesus by the grace of God. We lived in this world until He took us out of this world.

Now, "For to me to live *is* Christ, and to die *is* gain" (Philippians 1:21). We have died to this world, yes, but we are resurrected in Christ Jesus!

Free Will

Whenever I hear the term *free will*, I shudder! How vain. Who has bewitched you? Where will your will lead you? The Bible declares that God's children are led by the Spirit. C. H. Spurgeon stated, "Free will has carried many souls to hell, but yet never a soul to heaven."[8]

Is your trust in your election or His? Make sure of your salvation and trust in Him.

Many years ago, a preacher named John Wesley endeavored to give a sermon titled "Free Grace," in which he stated that God's free grace is offered to all men universally with the condition that they, by their own free will, accept this offer. Another preacher named George Whitefield sent Wesley a letter admonishing Wesley's carnal reasoning. Whitefield states, "Dear Sir, for Jesus Christ's sake, consider how you dishonour God by denying election. You plainly make salvation depend not on *God's free grace,* but on *man's free will.*" Free grace then would not be free or unmerited; God would have to look to man to have His work finished.

Whitefield goes on to state, "Free grace indeed. Free

---

8   Tom Carter, Compiler, 2200 Quotations from the Writings of Charles H. Spurgeon, Grand Rapids, MI: Baker Book House Co, 1988, 217.

not because free to all; but free, because God may withhold or give it to whom when He pleases."[9]

As I also have acknowledged, Whitefield said he might lose friends; however, rebuking false doctrine is found in preaching the truth in Christ.

Jesus himself, as well as Paul, preached against false doctrines of human likeness. Man would crucify the sovereign work of God in order to gloat and claim his rebellious free will.

Men believe it's their free will doing that which they do and also their perception that makes deeds good or evil. As Octavius Winslow said, "Who delivered up Jesus to die? Not Judas, for money; not Pilate, for fear; not the Jews, for envy; but the Father, for love!"[10]

Faith is not found in the will of man and neither is salvation; for these belong to our Lord.

Now remember, it's impossible to please God without faith, as stated in Hebrews 11:6 and faith is a gift from God. "For whatsoever is born of God overcometh the world: and this is the victory that overcometh the world, *even* our faith" (1 John 5:4). If born of God, then not of me.

The man who relies on his free will to find a saving faith is a man who glories in himself and attempts to take credit as he boasts of finding Jesus. This lost person is

---

9   Complete letter to John Wesley from George Whitefield can be found at spurgeon.org/~phil/wesley.htm.

10 Octavius Winslow, quoted by John Stott in, The Message of Romans, (Downer Grove, IL: IVP, 1994), 255.

deceived and deceives others. Today it's common to hear the phrase, I was born this way. I believe this is true. For we were all born in sin. But only by the grace of God are we saved.

At the point of regeneration, you are a new creature with a changed will. You are no longer a slave to the will of the flesh, but you are free now to do God's will.

Aye, the flesh is still there, but it is no longer your will, for your will is changed by the blood of Jesus. Yes, it is His righteousness in you.

Charles H. Spurgeon declared, "Free will I have often heard of, but I have never seen it. I have always met with will, and plenty of it, but it has either been led captive by sin or held in the blessed bonds of grace."[11]

Man's free will hit's head on with God's will, and it is God who controls the outcome.

The man enslaved to his own free will is carnal. "For to be carnally minded *is* death; but to be spiritually minded *is* life and peace" (Romans 8:6).

Many people believe Jesus is unable to save without man's cooperation. It is the Holy Spirit that brings conviction, and it is a humbling experience. Again we find God's will as the cause and effect and naught of man's free will. We are a work of God, born of God to His purpose. And yet many trust that the old man is somehow able to accept rather than receive, as though some glory belongs

---

11 Tom Carter, Compiler, 2200 Quotations from the Writings of Charles H. Spurgeon, Grand Rapids, MI: Baker Book House Co, 1988, 218.

to him. Remember, natural man is spiritually dead in his trespasses.

To deny free will is to deny self; the Arminian can do neither. Instead he declares himself either author or finisher but always the source of his own faith.

The Bible declares, "There is none that understandeth, there is none that seeketh after God. They are all gone out of the way, they are together become unprofitable; there is none that doeth good, no, not one" (Romans 3:11–12). So it is God who draws His elect to Him. It's to God's purpose and His glory: "And we know that all things work together for good to them who love God, to them who are the called according to *his* purpose" (Romans 8:28). We will see His purpose as we move through Bible doctrine. I know much will be interlocked, just as God's Word makes up a doctrine that binds His sheep together.

I overheard one Arminian say, "Well, I don't believe in this once saved and then go and do anything you want." It was all I could do to contain myself. My friend, you aren't truly saved if you are still doing your own free will. God's church is made up of children doing His will, not of those doing their free will. It is His love that keeps us, by grace through faith. Amen.

"For it is God which worketh in you both to will and to do of *his* good pleasure" (Philippians 2:13).

If you are one of His children, you will know His love, as Paul exquisitely states in Romans 6:14: "For sin shall not have dominion over you: for ye are not under the law, but under grace."

You say you know Him; do you believe Him? "For when ye were the servants of sin, ye were free from righteousness" (Romans 6:20).

Dearly beloved, it's a gift. "For the wages of sin is death; but the gift of God is eternal life through Jesus Christ our Lord" (Romans 6:23).

"But not as the offense, so also *is* the free gift. For if through the offense of one many be dead, much more the grace of God, and the gift by grace, *which is* by one man, Jesus Christ, hath abounded unto many" (Romans 5:15). The gift is not free will, rather it is free grace. Focus on your free will and you miss the mark. Free will is a natural attribute. Free grace is a super natural work of God in us. Natural man Adam or spiritual God/Man Jesus Christ? I've known both, and having received Jesus, I find God's grace irresistible!

The name of Jesus must surely strike fear in one believing salvation is found within man's will.

When we look at the sons of Abraham, Isaac and Ishmael, we find one legitimate (Isaac) and the other born after the flesh (Ishmael). "For it is written, that Abraham had two sons, the one by a bondmaid, the other by a freewoman. But he *who was* of the bondwoman was born after the flesh; but he of the freewoman *was* by promise" (Galatians 4:22–23).

So it was also with Cain, who was of the flesh, and Abel, who was of the Spirit.

Is your faith in your denomination and its doctrines, or is your faith in the object of faith, Jesus?

There is a war going on inside the regenerate, and Paul also addresses this. In Romans 7:17–25, Paul explains this war, which exists in all true believers.

> Now then it is no more I that do it, but sin that dwelleth in me. For I know that in me (that is, in my flesh,) dwelleth no good thing: for to will is present with me; but *how* to perform that which is good I find not. For the good that I would I do not: but the evil which I would not, that I do. Now if I do that I would not, it is no more I that do it, but sin that dwelleth in me. I find then a law, that, when I would do good, evil is present with me. For I delight in the law of God after the inward man: But I see another law in my members, warring against the law of my mind, and bringing me into captivity to the law of sin which is in my members. O wretched man that I am! who shall deliver me from this body of this death? I thank God through Jesus Christ our Lord. So then with the mind I myself serve the law of God; but with the flesh the law of sin.

That's why: it's the righteousness of Christ that saves us, not anything we do.

You may be chastised, but never cast out. Jesus himself declares in John 6:37, "All that the Father giveth me shall come to me; and him that cometh to me I will in no wise cast out."

There are three doctrines found in John 6:37:

1. The Father gives us to Jesus.

2. We come.

3. We have eternal security in Him.

Although we have been regenerated, the old man still lusts after the flesh. The essence of God's love is defined in 1 John 4:10, "Herein is love, not that we loved God, but that he loved us, and sent his Son *to be* the propitiation for our sins." Even though the child of God has a heart for Jesus, we must continue to grow in the Father's care and be led by the Spirit. We learn the reality of faith is obedience! That is our Father's will for us. He'll never forsake His children. He'll never leave us. It is all about love. "But God commendeth his love toward us, in that, while we were yet sinners, Christ died for us" (Romans 5:8).

Chapter 2

Any Means to an End

I would now like to address a saying I heard as a young lad. It simply is, "Any means to an end." I first heard it from a nun at a Catholic school I attended. I always believed it to be true, until God's Word proved it to be untrue.

The truth is that Jesus Christ is the means *and* the end! The means of man always becomes his end. That is, the means are more important than the end. Many churches use entertainment as the means and end. These are deceived by the vanity of their flesh. In today's churches, entertainment is used to market and bring crowds. Music is often used to sway and misguide individuals to a different gospel, one in which the means is more relevant and the true end cannot be achieved.

Church music has progressed in a worldly manner as a means for men to entertain men. Spiritual words mixed with worldly music are an abomination, as is mixing Christ Jesus with Santa.

> I hate, I despise your feast days, and I will not smell in your solemn assemblies. Though ye offer me burnt offerings and your meat offerings, I will not accept *them*: neither will I regard the peace offerings of your fat beasts. Take thou away from me the noise of thy songs; for I will not hear the melody of thy viols. But let judgment run down as waters, and righteousness as a mighty stream. Have ye offered unto me sacrifices and offerings in the wilderness forty years, O house of Israel? But ye have borne the tabernacle of your Moloch and Chiun your images, the star of your god, which ye made to yourselves. Therefore will I cause you to go into captivity beyond Damascus, saith the LORD, whose name *is* The God of hosts. (Amos 5:21–27)

They call their music "anointed" and then sell it, professing it is for God. They boast of their talent as a means to an end, but to what end?

If the music stopped only the true believers would stay to hear the sermon. As long as the excitement lasts, men stay.

We come by the Word of God and no other way! Many people quarrel over which music to play, and I have watched them entertain men. O, but they draw many.

This human, feel-good religion is focused on man instead of God. Remembering always, we come by the Word of God, not of ourselves, lest anyone boast. In truth, the worldly will use worldly means, because the Word says, "That which is born of the flesh is flesh; and that which is born of the Spirit is spirit" (John 3:6).

There are those who will wear any image and say it is for God, but in the end I have seen, as Paul saw, misuse of the Word of God to keep their act going. They have a means to their own ends and not to that of God.

In the third chapter of 2 Timothy, v. 9, Paul declares these people will be found out. They are the ones God addresses in Revelation 3:1, those who seem to be alive but are spiritually dead. They have little understanding of the Spirit of God, but they have a great understanding of the flesh and bring many in for *the show*. There are plenty of scripture verses describing those going through the motion, such as, Ephesians 6:6–7 "Not with eyeservice, as menpleasers; but as the servants of Christ, doing the will of God from the heart; With good will doing service, as to the Lord, and not to men:"

Scripture tells us how to worship spiritually. Psalms, hymns, and spiritual songs are in essence to be holy, respectful to God, not entertaining according to whatever man's current fads may be. For the most part, church services cannot be distinguished from secular shows. Many preachers will say any words to be heard.

God's church is made of Spirit, not of physical gifts but of spiritual gifts; not of physical men but of spiritual men, worshiping and singing as one body of Christ. God's church is not for money or self-gratification.

God hears the sweet voices, no matter what man hears as sweet. Those He predestined and has given the gift of a saving faith that no one may boast. Remember, the elect are a work of God. "For we are his workmanship, created in Christ Jesus unto good works, which God hath before ordained that we should walk in them" (Ephesians 2:10).

This (means to an end) is often used by the wolves disguised as sheep. They include preachers who become rich and important by selling their wares—by preaching a false gospel, one that even the humanist can endure. Beloved, listen closely. There is a difference between a true preacher of God and a charismatic preacher. One adheres to the Word; the other uses words to sway you in his direction. One is true emotion and the other is hype.

Humanists rely on charisma and think it is of God. For those without ears for God, do harken to the snake charmer. These preachers are more concerned about serving the will of man. Again, they have a look of holiness, but they preach a man friendly doctrine. They preach a Jesus Christ attainable by man's decision. They preach reliance upon man himself to be saved and to endure. Their worldly churches grow from their worldly knowledge as people are caught up in the preacher's degree and his ability to make them feel moved. Just putting the title "Doctor" or "Reverend" in front of one's name has nothing to do with being called by God, any more than the born-again experience can be a physical birth of flesh.

Once again we see the flesh of man at work, with no understanding of the Spirit of God who called the debased, the unschooled of this world, to be led by the Spirit of God.

Mega churches are built with mega dollars under the false assumption that these physical buildings are where God's children gather to worship in beautiful harmony. Although they claim that the church is the people, it's the sweetness of man and all his vanity that becomes clear as the Word becomes watered down and the end becomes clear by the means. It serves and worships man in many ways, disguised as worship of our heavenly Father.

While God is not a respecter of persons, these churches are. They show their finest and pat each other on the back, gloating on themselves in front of everyone. While praising the Lord, they build up their own self-esteem and vanity. After all; it's show time!

Unlike the apostles, living day by day, these imposters have a bright future as long as they stay worldly—as long as they water down God's Word and have a show of holiness according to man's will. It's for sure the man of God will be hated by the Pharisees, for the Pharisees' true love is this world. Power is begotten by money, and many will hear their message. But salvation is made sure by the election of the Lord. Only He can resurrect the dead, and they come only by His Word. Amen and Amen.

As we look deeper into natural man, we can see the true end of his means. Many, as God's Word says, come in the name of Jesus, but they are not of Him. Dressed as lambs, they are wolves disguised in humanism, having a show of holiness but only interested in *their* will being done. They are tares among the wheat.

Remember, if a man shows too much of himself, he reveals his own gospel and not that of the Christ, even though he uses the Bible. Being led by the Spirit, we point to Jesus. Many use the name of Jesus as a means to their own ends.

Some trick by healing, some by singing, and many by focusing on man's humanity. They use positive preaching for marketing instead of preaching the word of God. It is used by many humanists to create a man-friendly church. Nothing can take a person's mind off the spirit like the flesh. Most often the substitution goes unnoticed. Some ministries use a type of psychology that appeals to the worldly. The good news is the gospel of Jesus Christ, yet I hear more of the flesh and little of Spirit in these churches.

The elect of God have heard the Word of God and understand the stiff warnings of all the prophets who urged the people to turn to the Lord before it's too late. This warning comes from a loving Father who loves His children and warns of the antichrists of this world.

Paul spent much of his time rebuking these imposters.

Those who love this world and the darkness therein hate the truth. Therefore they claim we must change and be progressive in the twenty-first century. So they put a spin on the gospel or water it down, and make it friendlier as a means to an end. When confronted, they simply say, "Everyone translates it differently." Like the Pharisees their earthly livelihood depends on positive humanism. Their true belief is that the free will of man is needed instead of the will of God through His Word. And numbers mean success.

I sat in a Bible study and heard the question asked, "How can the Antichrist trick the world?"

I thought, "He already has tricked those who belong to this world." Even Christians get caught up at times, but *Jesus will deliver those of promise.* He chastises those who are His. Adultery toward God is rampant. They are adulterers who say, "I love you, Lord, but I need this life and all it has right now. Maybe later."

The reality of faith is obedience.

And now I would like to address the only means that God decrees as His means to the end. That means is the only door to heaven. It is of grace by a saving faith. Grace is a gift from God Himself, lest any boast of their choice or works done by them for their own salvation.

The way to heaven is through Jesus Christ, and is attained by those whom God has marked out beforehand. "It is the spirit that quickeneth; the flesh profiteth nothing: the words that I speak unto you, *they* are spirit, and *they* are life. But there are some of you that believe not. For Jesus knew from the beginning who they were that believed not, and who should betray him" (John 6:63–64).

If the law isn't able to save you—that is, keeping the law—what can? Only the grace of God, given to those He gives to His son. Augustine (354–430) Bishiop of Hippo, Africa and well known theologian said this concerning the free will of man, "I once laboured hard for the free will of man, until the grace of God at length overcame me."[12] The law itself is a good tutor, but the law is for the lawless. The elect of God are no more of the law but of grace. Because keeping the law is a physical and mental impossibility, those born of God come to Jesus. He is the only acceptable sacrifice for our sins. It is by His righteousness that we are made in His image. God gave the law through Moses, but grace is of God, and the means is His only begotten Son, Jesus Christ, our Savior. The children of God are led by the Spirit.

"For sin shall not have dominion over you: for ye are not under the law, but under grace" (Romans 6:14).

Remember this: the law is for the lawless and worldly, but grace is of God. It is a gift from God to those He foreknew. The law is physical, while God's grace is spiritual. The law is good in that it may be a deterrent for man from outward sin. But all will break it. If a man betrays his wife and commits adultery, the law won't stop him. But God's grace is of love, and love is able to do what

---

12 Calvin's Calvinism: treaties on the eternal predestination of God, 155.

the law can't do. What the law couldn't do, God's grace is sufficient to do. God is love. Grace therefore is the gift of love, a gift from God, for those sealed by the Holy Spirit until the day of redemption.

We come by the Word and no other means. Nevertheless, many preach a different gospel, just as they did in Paul's lifetime. "Let no man deceive you with vain words: for because of these things cometh the wrath of God upon the children of disobedience. Be not ye therefore partakers with them" (Ephesians 5:6–7).

How many different Bible versions are there? How many different religions? They are as politicians engaged in a war of words.

There is only one doctrine, it is found in the Word of God. But in each denomination, a doctrine of man is included to gain more converts—converts to their denominations, not to the Lord. Most of their congregants are confused, not knowing what they believe nor what their denomination believes. They know more about man's world because they are of this world. Thus, they use their own means, which are of their will, instead of the means of God's will, which is His immutable Word. The Bible declares that we come to God by the Word.

And then they boast, "Any means to an end."

Chapter 3

Going through the Motions

I have preached many sermons on *apathy*, which is indifference. These sermons always raised the hair on the backs of the necks of the tares. Why? Because they see themselves and feel my sermon was meant for them. They hate conviction; therefore they won't abide in God's Word.

Those who have ears for God will be convicted and repent. Those God draws near hear the Word and grow in faith. The tares, on the other hand, are full of hate and will murmur and have no change. They hate the messenger and reject the parts of the Word that could cause a change in their attitude.

You see, they are just going through the motions. Natural man's free will stems from his own pride. He is a slave, unable to forget himself. He goes through the motions because he is acting out this life. He is never at peace. His hope is in the present.

This is the way the tares live their lives. They are in motion with this world and the things of this world. They have no true discernment of the Spirit, only the flesh. "So then they that are in the flesh cannot please God" (Romans 8:8).

Man is led much by example. In the 1950's through the early 70's television depicted families as loving. Problems caused them to come together and be stronger. A few of these shows were *Father Knows Best, Leave it to Beaver, The Waltons,* and *The Andy Griffith Show.*

Yes, there was respect, and everyone knew his or her place within the family. Less confusion and a respectful love were predominant characteristics. These programs were great examples. The excitement was innocent and entertaining. Even cowboy and Indian movies weren't bloody. Like a good book, these shows made you think. Much was left to our imaginations.

Nowadays, movies do it all and call blood, guts, and explicit sex "entertainment." The truth is America is becoming like the movies, television, and the other entertainment we watch.

One of the effects of leprosy is the loss of feeling. You could hit a leper's fingers with a hammer, and he wouldn't feel a thing. I am sure many have become as lepers, unfeeling and numb. "Who being past feeling have given themselves over unto lasciviousness, to work all uncleanness with greediness" (Ephesians 4:19).

Remember your first love? How innocent. How fresh. Just holding hands was special. Nowadays young people are growing up so fast, with the help of the entertainment world and adults acting out parts with no emotion, that nothing is new or fresh or wonderful. Many young people go through the motions, never experiencing the depth of pure love.

I fear our senses are so dulled that we must have sensationalism to be entertained. Many people see today's shows as the norm and follow the examples put before them. We learn many worldly things in a monkey-see-monkey-do fashion. The Bible tells us that it is better not to even talk of these things.

Children's values used to come straight from their parents and those who cared about them. Nowadays, many parents act like children. Consequently, there are many children who have no one who loves and cares for them, so they look elsewhere. Maybe to television, possibly to anyone who pays attention to them, even if it costs them everything, including their lives. They become addicted to their world in the same way a rich man is addicted to his world. They are ready to give up eternity for the present.

Some actors, musicians, and athletes are teaching our young people how to behave badly, onstage and off. I remember my grandmother telling me to "beware of carnies." There are even some preachers using worldly means to deliver the spiritual Word, "Who changed the truth of God into a lie, and worshipped and served the creature more than the Creator, who is blessed for ever.

Amen (Romans 1:25). If the name of Jesus didn't come up every now and then, we might think we were at a talent show.

Even their good works are paraded on television for all to see and adore. God knows the hearts of the ones who are going through the motions for man to see.

In past years, young adults were told by their parents that sex was beautiful when two people were as one in marriage. A little later, many sex doctors simply left out the marriage part.

Before the grace of God was given to me, I went through the motions, trying to act out this life as it was shown to me. When I received Jesus Christ, I also received a change of heart, a new life that draws me even now, causing me to experience life more abundantly through the will of God.

Our only hope is in Christ Jesus. We are taught by God, not man. It's God's Word and His Spirit that lead His sheep. No more thinking that we are in control and our free will can save us. We, like Paul, are saved by the grace of God.

I once heard of a young man who wanted to be a basketball player, but he had one problem. He was more concerned with looking good on the court than making the basket. He wasn't putting his whole heart into it. Hence, he only went through the motions.

So many relationships people have today are untrue. Marriages for many are two people going through the motions. Everything about their life is temporal. They know nothing of the spiritual world of Jesus, the world for which He shed His blood. They live for the present and act out their parts as though they were under a contract that can be canceled at any time, usually by means of a lawsuit. Divorce seems now the norm. Many couples don't bother with getting married. Fathers leave their children because they are only willing to act like fathers as long as it is fun. Likewise, we often find that a mother's job and life come before her children. Frequently, we hear about mothers aborting their babies in the womb rather than nurturing this precious gift of life.

And how many sibling disputes have you seen? They are brothers and sisters in name only. They have not been taught the lesson of Cain and Abel or the lesson of Jacob and Esau. No, they have been taught by man and his traditions of pride to think, "I'm better than you."

And we are told, "This is the norm."

As a young sailor, I made two tours to Vietnam, stopping in different ports. I recall the drinking and the hollow eyes of people attempting to find some sort of fulfillment in life. It's the same today: natural man is going through this life with no feeling. He's going through the motions. Instead of being led by the Spirit, he is led by his own will, that which is not the will of the Father.

These not born again are dead in their trespasses. Without Christ Jesus, they are slaves to sin, not free. But when the Son sets you free, you are free indeed!

Churches are now more than ever like the government—that is, they are full of politics. Even many preachers preach politics, which are driven by money and power. They want many members and their money rather than a church that belongs to Christ.

Money and numbers to them are the worth of a church, and to get them, they must entertain. They go through the motions of a church but resort to humanism as their means and end.

These churches are like many marriages. They are acting out life instead of being true and passionate to their first love, the marriage of the Lamb. A man's night out or a lady's' night out is akin to a person who goes to church on Sunday and lives the rest of the week as though he doesn't belong to Jesus. What a night out says is, "I need my freedom from you." or "I'm committed, but not entirely."

Think about it. Do you fear losing your identity in this world and your free will by giving your whole self? If so, you are going through the motions. Can you truthfully say, "Jesus is my Savior and my faith is completely in Him. Start every day and end every day with Him."

From this love springs forth the love we have for others.

I remember when a prominent man committed adultery with a young woman. Instead of condemning this act, the world declared him only human and said any man would do the same, given the opportunity.

Before God's grace was given to me, I felt the same way. Truly a change of heart has come to a sinner, and repentance comes also with this new nature.

So, worldly men, you may go through the motions and enjoy the free will you desire so that God doesn't save you from yourself. Instead of being a servant to God, you serve yourself and he who keeps you slave—he who is known as the "Father of Lies." You serve one or the other.

Those of this world murmur and scoff. They always have. They complain while boasting of their shame. Any joy is short-lived, and in the end there can be no joy, only death. The Bible says that to God they have the aroma of death, but those not perishing have the aroma of Jesus Christ.

Natural man has no understanding of the Spirit; thus he will only go through the motions. A natural man will display apathy toward God, or possibly a look of holiness for men to see, but for sure inside there lies his true feelings: a hate for the doctrine of God. The natural man must change the Word to fit his life because there has been no change in him.

Chapter 4

The Gray Areas

We've all heard of the gray areas. They are the parts between right and wrong, good or evil. This is where most people are most secure because they feel in control of their free will. It's the part where we justify what we do by our own standards. People are comfortable because, in a gray area, they are their own persons.

In reality, they are lukewarm: neither cold nor hot. Scripture declares these people are especially disliked by God. Paul says of them, "Having a form of godliness, but denying the power thereof: from such turn away" (2 Timothy 3:5). The Bible says they are tossed to and fro.

I've found most people are more concerned with looking good to others rather than serving God. In serving God: if you think me a fool, let me be a fool for God.

We must understand that within the gray areas is where lies and deceit congregate, driven by human pride. These are where Satan uses his wolves disguised as sheep to further his agenda. These are no-man's-lands even to new Christians.

Many people find the most comfort and feel safest in the middle. Why would a child of God be so timid? "Let us therefore come boldly unto the throne of grace, that we may obtain mercy, and find grace to help in time of need" (Hebrews 4:16).

Now understand this! The wheat, who are the elect of God, will grow spiritually and be drawn to the light by God. Jesus is our light. The wheat will endure and grow until the harvest. As the elect grow in Christ, the gray areas will for them become less and less. Truth and light will guide them on their journey home. "For whom he did foreknow, he also did predestinate *to be* conformed to the image of his Son, that he might be the firstborn among many brethren" (Romans 8:29).

Conviction used to be a bad word to me. But it was conviction that brought me to repentance! The Holy Spirit convicts: He shows us our guilty nature, which causes repentance in the unregenerate. Washed in the blood of Jesus Christ and fully justified, our gray, dirty areas become whiter as we grow in the image of Jesus. We see the Spirit showing us Jesus. The old man, our flesh, is no longer able to toss us to and fro. Although the race is not finished, the true believer is changed by the grace of God, thus no longer desiring to sin.

Before being regenerated, he couldn't help himself. Now his will is to do the will of God. No longer a slave to sin, he is free indeed. Even though a man thinks himself good, he is blinded by pride.

Pride is at the root of all sin, and yet I hear so many boast of it these days, thinking it an attribute. God's children give themselves up and no longer are driven by their own will. The Bible declares, "For all that *is* in the world, the lust of the flesh, and the lust of the eyes, and the pride of life, is not of the Father, but is of the world" (1 John 2:16). A man full of pride will never succumb to God, except God choose him. Natural man has his pride in his flesh; spiritual man has faith in Christ Jesus.

You see, those born of God put their faith in Christ, who is able to make straight the path to heaven. Natural man is able to see only as far as pride allows, and this will lead him to his home, where his hellish father awaits.

The Narrow Road

The narrow road is a road followed by God's
    sheep,
led by the Good Shepherd.
It is white, spotless, and on good ground.

The wide road is a bending road followed
    by the goats, led by the Father of Lies.
It is this gray area where men stumble, and
    all hope dies.

At this present time of economic and social confusion, people seem to struggle to find answers to their immediate problems. Recently, almost everyone I've talked to has said the same thing: we're all in the same boat. They say this so as to feel safe. Safety in numbers is their constant.

This too is a form of staying in a gray area with no answers, no truth to set them free, and no understanding of God's love and purpose. Truth is; we aren't all in the same boat. The children of God are in the ark. Just as Noah was saved to God's purpose, so are the beloved. Look toward the rainbow, which is the kingdom of God!

Our hope is focused on Jesus Christ, not our free will, for our treasure is in heaven. I am aware that a man of this world, even while he sits in church or plays another round of golf, can't see or hear the truth of this matter. He will always, by his own free will, which is indeed not truly free, choose the present over the future. In the parable of the wheat and tares, Jesus Christ sets forth the undeniable truth that we all start out the same. You might say we are in the same boat. As we grow, the tares will try to choke out the wheat. However, God's election will stand.

A man named Thomas Bradwardine (1290 - 1349) an English cleric and a noted philosopher once said. "What multitude, O Lord, do this day join hands with Pelagius in contending for free will and in fighting ... free grace."[13]

Do you remember Cain and Abel? Abel's offering was

---

13 cprf.co.uk/quotes, Covenant Protestant Reformed Church

accepted and pleased God, but Cain's offering was, as Jude 1:12 puts it, "as clouds without water," an empty cloud.

The gray areas that man so dearly holds on to are merely a way to justify the sins he lives in. It seems to man a little thing, not worth much consideration. Little sins of little consequence. Dead is dead! If you aren't for Him, you are against Him. King David didn't even consider his sin with Bathsheba. No big deal! But when he was made to see his sin, he cried out with conviction, "I have sinned against the LORD" (2 Samuel 12:13).

For a child of God, there comes not only conviction, but also nurturing from the Holy Spirit, who leads us to Christ. And so we are obedient to the will of God. "For as many as are led by the Spirit of God, they are the sons of God" (Romans 8:14).

This life for the believer becomes progressively more black and white as the Holy Spirit convicts and causes the believer to grow spiritually. "He shall glorify me: for he shall receive of mine, and shall shew *it* unto you" (John 16:14). He understands this new life comes from the death, death on the cross.

Born again, the *new man* has a *new will*—a will of God for God, no longer in bondage to Satan but now free in Jesus. No longer lukewarm, the believer comes as a sinner and receives faith, trusting in Jesus by the grace of God. And all this is a free gift to the elect, who are given to Jesus by our heavenly Father.

We die to this world and live for God, obeying His will for us. We give up self, as did the Father's first fruit, Jesus.

Instead of plodding or simply going through the motions of life, the believer experiences a true and real change. With this change comes life more abundantly. Growth is life. Those who don't grow in the Spirit will die the second death. Many churchgoers never have grown and are stymied by the tares. Others may still be on the road to Damascus, not yet knowing Jesus Christ. God's will be done, in His time, for He alone is in control.

Many people in churches are wolves that hide their hearts well. They stalk the sheep as predators and hide among the wheat. To be sure, spiritual growth is light that these wolves can't stand. To exist, they must do their best to keep the sheep in the dark.

But the light of Christ will prevail, for light is truth, and we are led by His Holy Spirit.

Chapter 5

Accepting or Receiving

This chapter must again address man's pride and will
to be in control. "For who maketh thee to differ *from
another*? and what hast thou that thou didst not receive?
now if thou didst receive *it*, why dost thou glory, as if
thou hadst not received *it*?" (1 Corinthians 4:7).

*A*cceptance denotes the power of rejection by man; thus,
man is implied to have the ability to resist or change
what God has foreordained. God's children are the elect of
God; not that God is elected by the children. Romans 9:11
says, "(For *the children* being not yet born, neither having
done any good or evil, that the purpose of God according
to election might stand, not of works, but of him that
calleth;)" And in the same chapter, verse 16, "So then *it
is* not of him that willeth, nor of him that runneth, but of
God that sheweth mercy."

Think about it: Did Israel choose God?

Did the apostles choose Jesus?

Did Paul choose Jesus?

Three different Bible translations of John 3:27 proclaiming God's Sovereignty:

» "A man can receive nothing, except it be given him from heaven." King James Version

» "A person cannot receive even one thing unless it is given him from heaven." English Standard Version

» "A person can receive only what is given them from heaven." New International Version

Each of us must look deep into our own hearts and realize that if we are saved and know for sure we are going to heaven; it is a work of God—not of our will, but His. We were and are drawn to God by unmerited grace. If you are changed, give Him the glory!

Scripture never says God's grace is bestowed upon good people of good works because He knew from the beginning what they would do. Never does it say that!

Instead, the doctrine declares He knew us from the beginning, before anything we do. This addresses God's love and grace, not works.

"According as he hath chosen us in him before the foundation of the world, that we should be holy and without blame before him in love: Having predestinated us unto the adoption of children by Jesus Christ to himself, according to the good pleasure of his will" (Ephesians 1:4–5).

The most cited commentary on the Bible is probably that of Matthew Henry. He is quoted even by Arminians. Listen to him speak of free will: "The councils and decrees of God do not truckle to the frail fickle will of man."[14]

God told Jeremiah in 1:5, "Before I formed thee in the belly I knew thee; and before thou camest forth out of the womb I sanctified thee, *and* I ordained thee a prophet unto the nations."

For the elect, it's not a matter of accepting. The experience of receiving Jesus is undeniably a work of God in us. It happens. He calls and we come.

Charles Spurgeon understood God's grace when he said, "A man is not saved against his will, but he is made willing by the operation of the Holy Ghost. A mighty grace which he does not wish to resist enters into the man, disarms him, makes a new creature of him, and he is saved."[15] To God's children, it is our new position in Christ!

When you were born, you didn't accept your parents. It was your position as their baby that mattered. Born-again babes in Christ are sons of God and heirs to heaven by God's will.

---

14 cprf.co.uk/quotes, Covenant Protestant Reformed Church

15 Tom Carter, Compiler, 2200 Quotations from the Writings of Charles H. Spurgeon, Grand Rapids, MI: Baker Book House Co, 1988, 90

The word *receive* is used to help us understand that we were dead in our trespasses and were *unable* to accept. Only God can resurrect the dead. Man is passive.

Does this make a man less of a man? The answer is no, because now we are born of God unto belief in Jesus. John 3:3 declares that we must be born again. Being born again means everything is new, and that includes a new heart, a new attitude, and a new will. Being of God, we now are taught by God. The Bible says that no man seeks God. It's because they can't. Only after the gifts of God, grace and a saving faith, can we receive Jesus Christ. Only believers seek God, those born again and made alive in Christ Jesus.

The Bible is quite clear and always refers to us receiving. Before this unmerited favor, which is God's grace, was given to us, we could not please God, no matter how much we said we accepted Him. Even our faith is a gift of His who is the author and finisher of it.

Many preach that man's faith comes before or works together with God's grace, but hear Ephesians 2:8: "For by grace are ye saved through faith; and that not of yourselves: *it is* the gift of God:" By grace through faith. It's a gift. The word *it* used here refers to salvation. Faith in Jesus is given us as a channel unto God.

And in verse 10 are found four great doctrines: "For we are his workmanship, created in Christ Jesus unto good works, which God hath before ordained that we should walk in them."

1. We are a workmanship of God
2. Created in Christ Jesus
3. Unto good works
4. Ordained by God beforehand

Many churches make man the subject of a faith that man cannot produce. They preach a false doctrine that man shares in the work of God, thereby diminishing the power and will of God. It is a trick of the devil that uses man's pride to reject the truth.

Can I accept death? And yet it comes. Neither can I accept life everlasting of my own will. It's in God's hands. He is in control. We didn't control our first, physical birth, and we won't control our second birth. We can receive it, but only if it is the will of God. To His purpose, so His election might stand.

Do you hear? He calls. Is it you He calls? Is He drawing you near? He changes our desires. He changes our will. When He calls, you will know it, for you will truly know Jesus.

Just as the gray area diminishes, so faith grows, much like a mustard seed. God's grace is the cause of the new birth from which we receive Jesus in our hearts. We are a new creature, born of God, given to Jesus, promised to Him in the marriage of the Lamb. And our Lord never breaks His promises.

Romans 10:9 is used by many as a doctrine to lead man to Christ. However, they forget the second part of this passage, which says: You must believe it in your heart. Unless God's grace through faith has been given to you, you may say it all day long, but the work of the Holy Spirit will be missing. Try as you may, your will cannot be done. "But as many as received him, to them gave he power to become the sons of God, even to them that believe on his name: Which were born, not of blood, nor the will of the flesh, nor the will of man, but of God" (John 1:12–13).

Your salvation is of the Lord. It is Jesus' righteousness, which is the righteousness of God. It is not our righteousness in cooperation with his. Christianity brings everything like that to an end when it speaks of the righteousness of God. It is God who stands center. All man's efforts miss the mark.

> And be found in him, not having mine own righteousness, which is of the law, but that which is through the faith of Christ, the righteousness which is of God by faith. (Philippians 3:9)

> For therein is the righteousness of God revealed from faith to faith: as it is written, The just shall live by faith. For the wrath of God is revealed from heaven against all ungodliness and unrighteousness of men, who hold the truth in unrighteousness. (Romans 1:17–18)

In the epistle to the Romans, Luther saw the clarification of God's righteousness. He wrote, "God certainly desires to save us not through our own righteousness, but through the righteousness and wisdom of someone else or by means of a righteousness which does not originate on earth, but comes down from heaven."[16]

Many think themselves righteous and wise by their own free will decision, instead of God's righteous and wise election. They boast of their shame. In Hebrews 12:2, we are told to look to Jesus as "the author and finisher of *our* faith." If you have truly received Jesus Christ as Lord and Savior, you already know it wasn't by choice.

Charles Spurgeon, who is still known as the "prince of preachers," said, "It very often happens that the converts who are born in excitement die when the thrill is over." [17]That walk to the front of the church, by which many say they accept Jesus, never saved anyone. Only by being born again did you receive Him, and never before. Looking back, I know I was drawn to Him by our heavenly Father.

A. W. Tozer (1897–1963) an American Christian pastor, said, "Don't come down here at the altar and cry about it. You go home and live it."[18]

---

16 Commentary On Romans, Translated by J. Theodore Mueller, Kregel Publications, 28

17 C. H. Spurgeon, The Soul Winner, Whitaker House, 14.

18 oChristian.com, A. W. Tozer Quotes, 5

Dearly beloved, if a preacher isn't adhering to the Word of God, he is an antichrist. My prayer is that you not put faith in your own decision; rather, put your faith in Christ Jesus. God's promise is sure, and the Holy Spirit always leads us to Jesus. The Holy Spirit seals us to the day of redemption. You can be sure if Jesus calls there will be a change.

It is the Father who gives us to Jesus. And if you find yourself on your knees, it is because He calls for you. His call is irresistible to the chosen. Are you drawn to Jesus? Have you accepted Him on your terms without real change, or have you received Him as Lord and Savior?

Sure, I accept, but only because I have received Him. It's more irresistible than anything else. I am what I am by the grace of God. The reality of faith is obedience. Only the elect are obedient to that call. We come as sheep to the will of the Shepherd. He provides all for His sheep. He is the Bread of Life, the drink that satisfies. He is the staff of our salvation, and He is life itself. It is He who sustains us. Let us glorify Him.

Cross of Wood

True freedom and free will
Live far apart
Which do you treasure?
Ask your heart

Pray to Jesus; He has the answer
One is life, the other is cancer
Within my members lie pain and sorrow
And yet with joy I await tomorrow

So many say they accept, but
He came to me as I wept
I fought this freedom as best I could
Still He made me free with a cross of wood

Chapter 6

The Golden Calf
(Idolatry and Adultery)

66 "When ye have transgressed the covenant of the LORD your God, which he commanded you, and have gone and served other gods, and bowed yourselves to them; then shall the anger of the LORD be kindled against you, and ye shall perish quickly from the good land which he hath given unto you" (Joshua 23:16). Aaron made an idol in the form of a golden calf for the Israelites to worship; it was destroyed by Moses. Our Lord will destroy the false idols in a Christian's life, just as he used Moses to destroy the golden calf that Aaron made. "Do we provoke the Lord to jealousy? are we stronger than he?" (1 Corinthians 10:22).

An idol is used to refer to anything that is worshiped

other than God. Everyone has a god. A god is your first love, your true love. A god is what you hold most dear. A god is what you worship. A god isn't necessarily a person. In the Old Testament, pagans worshiped many gods.

Many people put more credence in a church building than in godly worship. Making a church building a golden calf is as common as making your faith the object of your worship. Many people actually grade a church by how beautiful the building looks and or the number of seats filled by bodies. These people boast of man's good works instead of Christ's work on the cross. A look of holiness becomes more important to some because they worship self-esteem and being looked up to. They don't see the golden calf, because they are full of their own self-righteousness.

Idolatry can be hidden so deep that it is seen as good. Humanism and the measurements of man mislead many. In their confusion, people may redefine the very term *religion*.

Idolatry is what unbelievers do. They substitute for God and worship the sinful lusts of this world, actually bringing the world into the church. It is because this world is all they know. How can someone truly love that which he cannot discern, let alone know? His emptiness can only be temporarily filled with a false hope that can't last. These feelings can come tangibly or emotionally; however, both end in sadness and death.

In the end, they won't last because man's will changes and as often as his free will changes, so do his idols. Man's will changes daily, if not by the second. Your free will cannot save you or keep you, but God's will can and does. Man simply can't rely on himself to sustain faith.

God's will is immutable. His decree is forever. Nothing can keep the beloved from Him. "For I am persuaded, that neither death, nor life, nor angels, nor principalities, nor powers, nor things present, nor things to come, Nor height, nor depth, nor any other creature, shall be able to separate us from the love of God, which is in Christ Jesus our Lord" (Romans 8:38–39).

This is very strong language and eloquently describes our Father's love, power, and resolve for His sheep. And I believe Christ's words on the cross describe every true believer's heartfelt desire to cry out, "Father, into thy hands I commend my spirit."

Dearly beloved, listen closely. Idolatry is adultery, in that many of those who claim to love Him are saying to God, "I have another," by their actions and thoughts.

The man who commits idolatry and says he loves God is the same as the man who commits adultery against his wife, but worse. Neither God nor the wife is his first love. No; for his first love is found within himself. He is a child of a liar and a murderer. He is led by the father of confusion and tossed to and fro by Satan himself. "If therefore ye have not been faithful in the unrighteous mammon, who will commit to your trust the true *riches*? (Luke 16:11).

There can be nothing he holds dear except the illusion he is doing God's will by doing his own free will. But the harsh reality is that it is his father the Devil whose will is being done. I say these strong words for the sake of any listening, that they be convicted by the Holy Spirit.

As the Bible declares, "You can't serve two masters." It comes down to whose will you are doing. While man believes in his free will, he in truth does the will of his father. In the end, you know who your father is by whose will it is you do.

Who do you serve and worship? Is it the music you seek? Is it the admiration and fellowship of others? Dwell and meditate on His precepts. The golden calf is found in deception, which is death. In Jesus there is peace and life everlasting. I beg you to close your eyes and listen to His Word. Turn the world off and draw nigh to Jesus.

Chapter 7

Focusing
(It Only Matters If You Care)

The subject of focus is a great divider. What we focus on tells so much about ourselves—our thoughts, attitudes, core values, motives, and even who or what we worship. Many do a good job of covering up their true selves, as we have discussed in earlier chapters. They go through the motions and hide in sheep's clothing. Only God can separate the tares from the wheat. He gathers His sheep.

Many fool themselves, for their hearts are able to deceive even their consciousness. Nonetheless, God draws His elect to Jesus. The elect have a change of heart, and yes, even their will changes, born free to serve God. They are able to see themselves as they really are, and it's not a pretty picture.

If you are a Bible student, remember with me a certain picture. We see in Zechariah chapter 3 the high priest Joshua standing before the Lord. Filthy rags represent the state our souls are in. We are guilty with no excuses. Our aroma is worse than garbage. And yet, for the chosen, that unmerited favor called God's grace is in these words spoken in the last part of verse 4: "Behold, I have caused thine iniquity to pass from thee, and I will clothe thee with change of raiment." Led by the Spirit, we are able not to sin.

Remember again your first love, how you spent most of your time with that person. And when you weren't with your love, your mind was preoccupied with thoughts of love and how the future was going to be. Together forever! Amen.

Well, imagine having that feeling along with peace in your heart, knowing for sure this love is the one that is forever. To those who are Christ's, He is our first love. He is our Alpha and Omega. He never deceives and is always faithful. This love is the most spiritual experience we can ever know. You might not believe my experience with Christ, but I can't deny it! Augustine states "And who is he that knows himself and says, "This is false," unless he himself is lying? But, because "love believes all things"—at least among those who are bound together in love by its bonds—I confess to Thee, O Lord, so that men may also hear; for if I cannot prove to them that I confess the truth, yet those who ears love opens to me will believe me."[19]

---

19 Thomas Nelson Publishers, Nelson's Royal Classics, Confessions St. Augustine, 203

The Bible declares that we have the mind of Jesus. With an understanding of this love, we now focus on Him. It's a wonderful feeling to be in His grace.

Only those born again by the grace of God are free, truly free to focus on the things above. Indeed, a spiritual war, but the new man who is born of God is no longer a slave to sin, worry, and all that this world has to offer. He now, because of his position in Christ, is able to be a conqueror instead of a victim in filthy rags. There is peace where there was worry, and grace has replaced the law in his heart—a law that he would never have been able to keep.

The old man is anxious and full of greed and worry. That is his life, and it keeps him focused on what he has. Sin abounds. He is deceived into believing this world is his treasure. Full of false hope and consumed with worry, he follows the lusts of the flesh and looks for any temporal island to give him pleasure and rest. He can't stay long though, because it's an ever-changing world, and although he grows old and weary, he must keep moving. He tires of the things he once desired. Finally, after much tossing and turning, he gives up the ghost, still feeling weak and unsatisfied, for the flesh profits nothing. His gods cannot save him.

Two false gods mentioned in the Bible are Gad, the god of luck, and Meni, the god of fate. Luck and fate are what the old man holds as truths. Evolution theories are built on these precepts.

Godless as Esau, natural man doesn't always know which god he worships and serves, as he has no understanding of that which he serves. In fact, he believes he serves himself by his own free will. Thus he is a slave to sin.

Earlier in this book, I mentioned attitude. I've heard it said that "Attitude is the paintbrush to your mind." That is, the way you perceive this world brings about your reactions. We must only look to God and our attitude about Jesus to find out what we focus on. I suspect many will find their focus more in tune with the world than with our Savior. Instead of coming as sinners, dead in their trespasses, many try to come as righteous by their own free will and faith in cooperation with the Creator. Only Jesus has the power. Man can add naught to salvation.

Many people go to church and they defend their love for Christ in front of Christians; this is true. They defend as far as their faith will allow. For many, faith would not show up without the music.

What did Jesus bring? What was Paul's message if not Christ crucified? Where was their beautiful church?

The true church will be focused on Jesus and preaching the Word, in season and out. The true beauty of a church is the light within.

Without entertainment, many preachers wouldn't have a ministry. I know it is impossible to reach any but God's beloved when one is armed only with His truth, that being His Word. "For the preaching of the cross is to them that perish foolishness; but unto us which are saved it is the power of God" (I Corinthians 1:18).

To truly focus on the things above, we must put on the new man. The new man is led by the Spirit, having had a true change of heart. He possesses a new attitude and a heart for God. He makes time for God, focusing on His love for us.

At the very heart of all worship is the sermon. It cannot be a sermon without understanding that we are here to worship the slain Lamb. It's in the name of Jesus we pray and in His blood we are washed and made clean for our Father in heaven.

Listen more to His Word and less to the harps of men. We should all sing together, not calling attention to ourselves. Spiritual blessings are for the body of Christ and not entertainment. Herein we find a peace and joy like no other.

As a church, I pray we never peddle our goods as did the market changers of past days. "For the scripture saith unto Pharaoh, Even for this same purpose have I raised thee up, that I might shew my power in thee, and that my name might be declared throughout all the earth" (Romans 9:17).

And I ask you again, "For who hath resisted His will?" (Romans 9:19).

Understand the Devil mimics and gives man a temporary, false hope in this world. Man, being deceived just as in the Garden of Eden, is prey to be devoured by Satan.

Worldly man has Santa at a time the man of God worships Jesus. "But," say you, "I have both."

Then I say, you can't serve two masters. How does a pagan day serve God?

At this many will walk away holding on to this world. Humanism to these seems right.

If everything the world has to offer was lost, and you had nothing left, could you know His love, His power, and His will for you? "For what is a man profited, if he shall gain the whole world, and lose his own soul?" (Matthew 16:26).

The new man lives as an alien in this world. This is not his home. Even with the worldly riches he has, a Christian will not focus on this world. He yearns to be with his Father in heaven. "But ye *are* a chosen generation, a royal priesthood, an holy nation, a peculiar people; that ye should shew forth the praises of him who hath called you out of the darkness into his marvelous light" (1 Peter 2:9). For these peculiar people, earthly treasure will not become the golden calf. It is only temporal. To be a good steward, a man must focus on the things above. This world is never able to satisfy man's desire to taste everything. Blaise Pascal called it "licking the earth."[20] A child of God is content in the sweetness of Jesus. "O taste and see that the LORD *is* good: blessed *is* the man *that* trusteth in him" (Psalm 34:8).

Our focus is on Jesus. A matter of Spirit versus flesh, life or death. God's will be done on earth as it is in heaven. Meditate on this. Turn to Jesus; you have the aroma of the Son. But if you are focused on this world, you have the aroma of those who are perishing. Who has bewitched you?

---

20 Blaise Pascal, Pensees, #666

For those of the flesh, the motto is, "let us eat and drink; for to morrow we shall die" (Isaiah 22:13). But for those led by the Spirit, I say, "O death, where *is* thy sting?" O grave, where *is* thy victory?" (1 Corinthians: 15:55).

Of course, many can't understand the foolishness of God, for they are the ones drawn by other gods. This world of flesh is their god, and the Devil is their master. "But God hath chosen the foolish things of the world to confound the wise; and God hath chosen the weak things of the world to confound the things which are mighty; And base things of the world, and things which are despised, hath God chosen, *yea*, and things which are not, to bring to nought things that are: That no flesh should glory in his presence" (1 Corinthians 1:27-29).

Don't be fooled by earthly wisdom or by the holy look of humanism. For sure they see themselves as right. Their power is in their pride. After all, they think themselves the wisest of this world. Not drawn to Jesus, they turn to fads and fables. They are always learning, but never able to discern the truth. Misguided, their focus is on the humanism of man instead of the theism of God. Old man's desire is the importance of his will; the new man's desire is doing the will of God.

In the scheme of things, men dwell on what is most important to them. They talk about their favorite subjects the most. My favorite subject used to change as the seasons changed. They were short-lived dreams at best. These loves were built on sand. They were poured out as my life was being poured out. James says our life here is just a mist, meaning our time here is short.

Our focus is always on what we perceive as our reality. This can make us joyful or sad, but it only matters if we care. The elect receive joy, in that this is not our home. God's Word will endure. Jesus Christ is our cornerstone; He is the Rock of our salvation. The true church is not built on a rock of man that will die. No, the Rock our house is built upon is Jesus Christ, our living Savior. Reality to those perishing is death, but to the chosen it is life everlasting. This life is not the end for the beloved, but merely a journey by which we are purified by the propitiation of our Savior, Jesus Christ. Focus on the Lamb of God. The reality of faith is obedience. How can we say we love Him when our focus is steadfast on this world and ourselves?

Examine your heart. Only you and God know your heart. What thoughts do you entertain? Many feel sorry for what they don't have or feel that they have been slighted. These people are full of pride.

Others are able to feel empowered when their good works are seen by this world. These people can't get enough, for praise is their reward, here and now.

But here and now won't last. God's church doesn't rely on their good works. One man said he is assured of his salvation by his ministry. The same man says also that a man can lose his salvation. He looks to works as a means or way to God.

Satan deceives, and the one being deceived continues

the deception. True believers focus on the saving work on the cross—a work only Jesus was able to do. Give the Lord all praise.

His children don't trick others into believing by saying, "Any means to an end." There is only one way. We come by the Word of God. God uses spiritual seed, not physical seed, for the beloved. Everything changes, but not the Word. You can't nourish the spirit with the world that will pass away.

What I'm saying is, don't bring every worldly fad that comes along and join it to God. Instead stay focused on the Word of God!

Held within the Word, you will find His doctrine, not that of man. You will find His will, not your will. You will find His love for those He foreknew, predestined, called, justified, and glorified. And His sheep will be drawn to the Lamb of God.

Chapter 8

Natural Man
(Man of Flesh)

When I was dead in my trespasses, I overlooked many people and many things in life. What I was focused on was my will. Anything else I considered in my way. And as I stated earlier, I believed in any means to an end.

Now I confess before God and man, "I am a sinner! I was a victim of my circumstances and of other people. But now, no longer am I a victim, but a conqueror in Christ."

For the great Shepherd heard my cry, and I heard Him call.

Screaming and Crying

I lay in the womb
With no understanding,
Dark but warm I thought it home

Suddenly, in the wink of an eye
Hands grasped me 'bout my thigh
I fought and strived to stay inside
But no use, I wrestled like Jacob
Alas, I lost but won

Yes, screaming and crying came I
Came screaming and crying, thought I was
    dying
And I was dying, dying to this womb, this world
No longer I, but He
No longer bondage, but free

Irresistible is his love for me
Out the womb that I may see
I said, "Lord, how can this be?"

His answer was brief
"Because before I formed thee
I gave thee belief"

Before, I enjoyed the temporal lusts of this world.
Living in darkness and unable to truly know love, I lived
only in the flesh and by the law.

Peter describes the flesh in this way: "For all flesh *is* as grass, and all the glory of man as the flower of grass. The grass withereth, and the flower thereof falleth away:" (1 Peter 1:24).

And 1 John 2:15 states, "Love not the world, neither the things *that are* in the world. If any man love the world, the love of the Father is not in him."

Dearly beloved, there are many sitting in pews, going through the motions, and dying in their trespasses. They seek to glorify themselves. Self-righteous, they hold God's Word and His preachers up to ridicule. "As we said before, so say I now again, If any *man* preach any other gospel unto you than that ye have received, let him be accursed. For do I now persuade men, or God? or do I seek to please men? for if I yet pleased men, I should not be the servant of Christ. But I certify you, brethren, that the gospel which was preached of me is not after man. For I neither received it of man, neither was I taught *it*, but by the revelation of Jesus Christ" (Galatians 1:9–12).

To these humanists, the Word must be changed or watered down to make it *man friendly*. They desire worldly fellowship even within the church, not understanding spiritual fellowship is a gift from God. The true church is a holy union of believers and in no way resembles this world of fads and pagan theatrics. I'm reminded of that old hymn, "Softly and Tenderly Jesus Is Calling."[21]

Because we have peace and fellowship with God

---

21 cyberhymnal.org/htm/s/o/sotlyat.htm

through His Son, we are able to have the same with our true brothers and sisters in Christ. As for the unbelievers, their compassion for man far exceeds their love for God. Unless they are in the entertainment business they fear they can't exhibit *their church* in a more worldly way. Natural men soothe their consciences by proclaiming that they do this for Jesus.

Many churches proclaim their programs and events in bold letters and focus on man's desires rather than on true and pure worship and the preaching of the Word of God, for His words sound strange and foreign to them. Their understanding and measure seems much wiser if one believes man comes to God by his own will.

> For it is written, I will destroy the wisdom of the wise, and will bring to nothing the understanding of the prudent. (1 Corinthians 1:19)

> For after that in the wisdom of God the world by wisdom knew not God, it pleased God by the foolishness of preaching to save them that believe. (1 Corinthians 1:21)

> Because the foolishness of God is wiser than men; and the weakness of God is stronger than men. (1 Corinthians 1:25)

These three verses address natural man, although they are written to the elect so they will have an understanding of the false doctrines of humanists. If a man has not godly wisdom, which can only come from God, and if a man cannot hear God, because God has not called him, then how can this man know or understand God? How can this man follow or trust God?

As always, we look to our Father for the answers. "For ye see your calling, brethren, how that not many wise men after the flesh, not many mighty, not many noble, *are called*: (1 Corinthians 1:26).

The wise of this world store up their treasure in this world. Their churches and synagogues are for this and of this world. The treasure of God's elect is in heaven.

"Henceforth I call you not servants; for the servant not knoweth what his lord doeth: but I have called you friends; for all things that I have heard of my Father I have made known unto you. Ye have not chosen me, but I have chosen you, and ordained you, that ye should go and bring forth fruit, and *that* your fruit should remain: that whatsoever ye shall ask of the Father in my name, he may give it you" (John 15:15–16).

Chapter 9

Spiritual Regeneration

In the gospel of John, chapter 3, verses 3 and 7, Jesus tells us we must be born again. Now, He doesn't say being born again is one option. He emphatically states there is no other way. As a matter of fact, in verse 6, He states, "That which is born of the flesh is flesh; and that which is born of the Spirit is spirit." Or, in other words, "That is, They which are the children of the flesh, these *are* not the children of God: but the children of the promise are counted for the seed" (Romans 9:8).

Those born of God are a workmanship of God.

Let us look again at John 1:13: "Which were born, not of blood, nor of the will of the flesh, nor of the will of man, but of God." Immediately, the idea that it was a decision wrought on by man's free will, man's faith, or any other way of man becomes false.

Yes, dearly beloved; it is God Himself who chooses, and it is by His sovereign purpose we are drawn to His Son, Jesus Christ.

If you are a child of God, you know it was by the grace of God drawing you near all along. The bride is given to the groom by the Father. "All that the Father giveth me shall come to me; and him that cometh to me I will in no wise cast out" (John 6:37).

No man has ever come to Jesus by his free will. "No man can come to me, except the Father which hath sent me draw him: and I will raise him up at the last day" (John 6:44).

After reading these verses, those who still believe in man's free will as a means needed for salvation should read John 6:63–65. "It is the spirit that quickeneth; the flesh profiteth nothing: the words that I speak unto you, *they* are spirit, and *they* are life. But there are some of you that believe not. For Jesus knew from the beginning who they were that believed not, and who should betray him. And he said, Therefore said I unto you, that no man can come unto me, except it were given unto him of my Father."

God's children neither give God's glory to man nor boast in themselves. We must adhere to God's Word and be obedient to Him.

Faith also is of God. It is not of man's will, as you have been told by false teachers. "For by grace are ye saved through faith; and that not of yourselves: *it is* the gift of

God: Not of works, lest any man should boast" (Ephesians 2:8–9).

Charles H. Spurgeon said that he, like many, started out believing as Arminians do—that he chose Jesus. But it became clear to him that God had been drawing him to Jesus all along. He describes his experience this way:

Well can I remember the manner in which I learned the doctrines of grace in a single instant. Born, as all of us are by nature, an Arminian, I still believed the old things I had heard continually from the pulpit, and did not see the grace of God. When I was coming to Christ, I thought I was doing it all myself, and though I sought the Lord earnestly, I had no idea the Lord was seeking me. I do not think the young convert is at first aware of this. I can recall the very day and hour when first I received those truths in my own soul—when they were, as John Bunyan says, burnt into my heart as with a hot iron; and I can recollect how I felt that I had grown on a sudden from a babe into a man—that I had made progress in Scriptural knowledge, through having found once for all, the clue to the truth of God. One week-night, when I was sitting in the house of God, I was not thinking much about the preacher's sermon for I did not believe it. The thought struck me, *'How did you come to be a Christian?'* I sought the Lord. *'But how did you come to seek the Lord?'* The truth flashed across my mind in a moment—I should not have sought him unless there had been some previous influence in my mind to make me seek him. I prayed, thought I, but then I asked myself, *How came I to pray?* I was induced to pray by reading the Scriptures. *How came I to read the Scriptures?* I did read them, but what led me to do so? Then, in a moment, I saw that God was at the bottom of it all, and that he was the Author of my faith, and so the whole doctrine of grace opened up to me, and from that doctrine I have not departed to this day, and I desire to make this my constant confession, 'I ascribe my change wholly to God.'[22]

Those who come to Jesus are the elect of God, lest they boast of their free will and their faith. The true believers boast in Him and are able to worship and offer up their works because their works are obedient to His will. Only by the grace of God can one give up self and pride.

In Romans 8:29–30, sometimes referred to as the golden chain, we are given God's plan of salvation from beginning to end. "For whom he did foreknow, he also did predestinate *to be* conformed to the image of his Son, that he might be the first born among many brethren. Moreover whom he did predestinate, them he also called: and whom he called, them he also justified: and whom he justified, them he also glorified."

This is God's decree: salvation according to His will and election. God is sovereign, and He is the Author of salvation. Many may try to change this doctrine to fit their desires, but it is He who has the key to open the door.

---

22 C.H. Spurgeon, The Early Years (Edinburgh: The Banner of Truth Trust, 1962), 164-165.

I beg you to read His Word very carefully and to be taught by God. Only His sheep will come. Only His sheep will joy in His will.

When we see God face-to-face, we shall know it is His love for us through the Lamb of God that has saved us. And when He asks us how we have come, we will reply, "By the blood of Jesus Christ." All glory to God!

Chapter 10

Works

"Even so then at this present time also there is a remnant according to the election of grace. And if by grace, then *is it* no more of works: otherwise grace is no more grace. But if *it be* of works, then is it no more grace: otherwise work is no more work" (Romans 11:5–6).

Recently, the Holy Spirit revealed to me the works by which we all will be judged. Until now, in Revelation 20:12–13, the phrase *"according to their works"* puzzled me greatly. Even the elect wouldn't want to be judged on their own works. It was right in the middle of a sermon, while making the point that you can't go to heaven by any worldly work of your own, that I was drawn to His truth.

Earlier Scripture in Ephesians chapter 2 declares, "For by grace are ye saved through faith; and that not of yourselves: *it is* the gift of God: Not of works, lest any man should boast. For we are his workmanship, created in Christ Jesus unto good works, which God hath before ordained that we should walk in them" (v. 8–10).

So, when asked, "What shall we do, that we might work the works of God?" Jesus answered, "This is the work of God, that ye believe on him whom he hath sent" (John 6:28–29).

This gift the elect receive is Jesus, and the work in us is His finished work on the cross. There is no boasting of faith, but glorying in the object of our faith, which is Jesus Christ, and giving thanks for the spiritual work done in us through Him. Born again, we are a workmanship of the Father.

While many are trying to work their way to heaven, because they don't truly believe in Jesus Christ, we are able to trust in His work on the cross. The people struggling to work their free will are trying to prepare a way. The way for the elect has been prepared by Jesus Christ, the Son of God. In Luke chapter 10, we are shown two sisters, Martha and Mary. While Martha worked and complained, her sister Mary listened to Jesus. One worked while one received Jesus that day. Mary was not concerned or confused by this world. Moral of this parable is to stop thinking of your good works and listen to Jesus. Good works will follow the work of Jesus. Instead of focusing on our work, focus on His work at Calvary.

It's very clear: some who do read the Bible and go to church still are unable to hear the truth. They simply incorporate their Jesus with this world. That is, they sew a new patch on an old garment. They put new wine in an old leather bottle. You can't serve two gods, for you will always love one more than the other.

Grace comes from God through faith in His Son. And this, dearly beloved, is the work of God. He calls His sheep and they come, being drawn by the Father, given to the Son, baptized in the Holy Spirit, and sealed unto the day of redemption.

Man's heart is where his treasure is. We are but sojourners here in a land that is not our home. The Bible says the flesh profits nothing. The work done by the flesh—that is, physical works—won't save. A wonderful singing voice or giving to the poor in and of themselves have no meaning and won't endure. It is the work done in you by God that perseveres. Praise be to Him!

Prayer

We follow Jesus in how we should pray. In Matthew chapter 6:9–13, "After this manner therefore pray ye: Our Father which art in heaven, Hallowed be thy name. Thy kingdom come. Thy will be done in earth, as *it is* in heaven. Give us this day our daily bread. And forgive us our debts, as we forgive our debtors. And lead us not into temptation, but deliver us from evil: For thine is the kingdom, and the power, and the glory, for ever. Amen."

And now that we have heard the word of God on how we are to pray, what shall we pray? "Likewise the Spirit also helpeth our infirmities: for we know not what we should pray for as we ought: but the Spirit itself maketh intercession for us with groanings which cannot be uttered. And he that searcheth the hearts knoweth what *is* the mind of the Spirit, because he maketh intercession for the saints according to *the will of* God" (Romans 8:26–27).

A person's true feelings and thoughts are not necessarily what he pray's about. Our thoughts many times just don't align with our prayers to God. Therefore, as this passage indicates the will of the elect is brought into subjection by the Spirit. "For the creature was made subject to vanity, not willingly, but by reason of him who hath subjected *the same* in hope, Because the creature itself also shall be delivered from the bondage of corruption into the glorious liberty of the children of God" (Romans 8:20–21). A man's heart will deceive but the mind of the Spirit is always truthful. As a young child growing up in the Catholic Church, I was told to go to confession. I often made up sins to tell the priest. I did this because I didn't want him to know the really bad sins that, as a Catholic, were called mortal sins.

Many praying aloud in churches, before people, pray that which they believe others want to hear. Just as I confessed the common sins but God knows our hearts.

And when thou prayest, thou shalt not be as the hypocrites *are*: for they love to pray standing in the synagogues and in the corners of the streets, that they may be seen of men. Verily I say unto you, They have their reward. But thou, when thou prayest, enter into thy closet, and when thou hast shut thy door, pray to thy Father which is in secret; and thy Father which seeth in secret shall reward thee openly. But when ye pray, use not vain repetitions, as the heathen *do*: for they think that they shall be heard for their much speaking. (Matthew 6:5–7)

Confessing to God, who knows me personally and knowing God personally, it is Jesus I confess and God's mercy I seek. "Who shall lay any thing to the charge of God's elect? *It is* God that justifieth. Who *is* he that condemneth? *It is* Christ that died, yea rather, that is risen again, who is even at the right hand of God, who also maketh intercession for us" (Romans 8:33–34). Pray in the Spirit; give Him the praise and glory.

I pray men stop boasting of their acceptance of Jesus and their work in front of others, understanding that God chose those of promise before the foundation of the world to receive His Son, who is the Christ.

No one can accept what he hasn't received. And only by receiving can he know Jesus. No one I know would resist being given a million dollars for free. Much the same God's sheep come, for His free grace is irresistible.

The carnal man who calls himself a Christian tries to justify himself by his own works, by his own free will. While Jesus should be the focus, camaraderie and entertainment are what the natural man has in common with the others at his church. A false believer going to a church has only a display of his so-called good works. His testimony is mostly about himself and the worldly things God has done in his life. Not being sober minded, he glories in himself while trying to convince himself and others that "This is for God."

Does our Lord see us lifting up our hearts to Him in psalms, hymns, and spiritual songs, making melody in our hearts or in the flesh as pagans do? Many churches follow the world in song. Do we respond to those with beautiful voices, or are all of God's children heard? Its inside, hidden from the world, that God knows His sheep. Instead of being beautiful, respectful, and holy, carnal music is full of leaven. It sounds good to the world because it belongs to the world.

Those of us who listened to the Beatles heard John Lennon declare that the Beatles were more popular than Jesus. While I liked the Beatles music, I always knew the beat was meant for man.

Many people say, "Listen to the words," but the beat is a powerful worldly rhythm. It causes them to stir emotionally rather than spiritually; it is meant to entice and seduce, even trick. Come in and join the fun. We'll entertain you and give you the Jesus of the world. Once again, we see man's will at *work*. So much importance is placed on good works that the church's carnal work becomes the end in itself, numbers instead of sound doctrine. "But if our gospel be hid, it is hid to them that are lost" (2 Corinthians 4:3).

In Psalms 46:10, we find Gods words "Be still, and know that I *am* God." The true work of God is hidden inside the temple of those understanding their helpless state, those that are meek and the quiet-as-a-lamb Christian. It is they who have received His will in their hearts having first received His grace. As did Joshua, these have been given victory in Christ Jesus.

"NOW faith is the substance of things hoped for, the evidence of things not seen" (Hebrews 11:1). Just as faith is not seen outwardly, neither are works of the flesh proof of Christianity. Only those born again have intimacy with Christ whereby they know Him. While He uses His own for His work, it remains, as we do, His work.

The children of God know that their home is in heaven and that it's already ordained by our wonderful Father. Yes, these already know they're going to heaven, because the Father has told them so in His Word. The Holy Spirit bears witness of Jesus in their hearts. It is finished. That good work in me is Jesus Christ. Love Him with all of your heart, mind, and soul. Put Him first in your thoughts and actions, for only He is righteous. Only He is worthy. Only He is able. Only He is God.

Thoughts

Within my books are many notes:

Because I read, I write.

Old man, follow the new man born of God.

Flesh knows flesh, but my spirit knows Jesus.

Think nothing of my scribbling, read God's
  Word.

Be of God's will or perish of your own will,
  which is not free.

Natural man, being in jail, submits to the
  jailer, but thinks himself a free man.

Hate is taking the wrong medicine.

A natural respect is fear, but a godly respect
  is love.

A man's free will falls short of God's will
for His elect

Out of necessity carnal men must justify
their sins by their will

Why do you do it? Carnal man declares, I
was born this way

Free will is natural; giving up that will is a
work of God

You say you believe in Jesus Christ, I ask
you, do you know him?

Natural man has his pride in the flesh;
Spiritual man has faith in Christ Jesus.

If we were only to read the words of Jesus
Christ written in our Bibles, we would
know God's will.

Free Will

Deep within I've often found
My dreaded will that would abound

If not for you, Lord, I could not see
How you loved and died for me

Lay waste this awful sin
Put to death my pride within

The mind of Jesus, my soul is free
And now I'm Yours, my destiny

My will was not free at all
But freedom came when I heard you call

When I was very young, my life was excellent and my health was superb. My parents, my siblings, and my time were all that grandeur could be. I took for granted every fresh breath and thought that these gifts of God would always be. Oh, there was good and bad, but I did not understand the evil within brought about long ago in Eden.

I always said, "Anyone could write a book if they ever had a thought."

Would my book demonstrate the bad? Or would I be compelled, drawn to tell of the love God has given me? Even with disappointment, He brings me joy in understanding His will.

As the Word of God declares, *"And we know that all things work together for good to them that love God, to them who are the called according to his purpose."* (Romans 8:28)

God is love and in His love we see Jesus. In His love is found His Spirit, which guides, counsels, and comforts.

For it is God which worketh in you both to
will and to do of His good pleasure.
—Philippians 2:13